Our Favori
Ground
Recipes

Copyright 2007, Gooseberry Patch
First Printing, April, 2007

Do the unexpected at dinnertime! Line a sombrero with
bandannas and fill with tortilla chips...perfect for munching
while waiting for Nachos Magnifico to bake.

Nachos Magnifico

Serves 6 to 8

1 lb. ground beef
1 c. onion, chopped
salt and pepper
2 15-oz. cans refried beans
4-oz. can diced green chiles
1 to 2 c. salsa
1 c. shredded Cheddar cheese
1 c. shredded mozzarella cheese

1 c. shredded Monterey Jack
  cheese
6-oz. container guacamole
2-1/4 oz. can sliced black
  olives, drained
1 c. green onion, chopped
1-1/2 c. sour cream
tortilla chips

Brown ground beef and onion in a large skillet over medium
heat; drain. Add salt and pepper; set aside. Spread beans in a lightly
greased 13"x9" baking pan; spoon beef mixture over top. Top with
chiles and salsa; sprinkle with cheeses. Cover and bake at 400 degrees
for 35 to 40 minutes. Top with guacamole, olives, green onion and
sour cream. Serve with warmed tortilla chips.

A large unfolded map makes a very clever table topper!
Sure to spark conversations about places you've been and
spots you'd like to visit.

Taco Dip

Serves 8

16-oz. pkg. pasteurized process
    cheese spread, diced
2 8-oz. pkgs. cream cheese,
    diced
16-oz. jar salsa

1-1/4 oz. pkg. taco seasoning
    mix
1 lb. ground beef, browned and
    drained

Melt cheeses in a slow cooker on low setting; set aside. While melting,
combine salsa, taco seasoning and beef; stir into cheese mixture. Heat
on low setting for 20 minutes, until hot and bubbly.

Mix & match different colors and patterns of place
settings, just for fun!

Tiny Pizzas

Makes 2 dozen

1 lb. ground beef
1 lb. ground sausage
16-oz. pkg. pasteurized process
   cheese spread, diced

1 T. dried oregano
1 loaf sliced party rye

Brown ground beef and sausage in a skillet over medium heat; drain.
Reduce heat; gradually add cheese, stirring until melted and well
mixed. Stir in oregano. Spread tablespoonfuls of mixture on each rye
slice; arrange on an ungreased baking sheet. Bake at 375 degrees for
15 to 20 minutes.

7

Brand new terra cotta saucers lined with parchment paper
make fun serving dishes for garnishes like chives
or bacon bits.

Southwest Potato Skins

Makes one dozen

6 potatoes
1 lb. ground beef
1/2 c. onion, chopped
1 t. salt
1 t. pepper
1-1/4 oz. pkg. taco seasoning
    mix

12-oz. pkg. shredded Cheddar
    cheese, divided
12-oz. pkg. shredded
    mozzarella cheese
Garnish: sour cream, chives,
    and bacon bits

Bake potatoes at 450 degrees for one hour, or until tender. Cut in half lengthwise and scoop out center of each potato, leaving 1/4 inch around edges. Save centers of potatoes for another recipe. In a large skillet, brown ground beef with onion, salt and pepper; drain. Add taco seasoning and heat through. Place potato halves on a greased 15"x10" jelly-roll pan; set aside. Combine cheeses; sprinkle half over potatoes. Top with ground beef mixture and remaining cheese mixture. Broil 3 to 4 inches from heat source until cheese is bubbly. Dollop with sour cream; sprinkle with chives and bacon bits.

A little red wagon makes a great carry-all for any
outdoor gathering. Fill it with crushed ice and bottles of
soda, water and juice boxes.

Mixed-Up Meatball Dip

Serves 24

1 lb. ground beef, browned and drained

1 lb. ground sausage, browned and drained

2 16-oz. pkgs. Mexican pasteurized process cheese spread, cubed

4 10-3/4 oz. cans cream of mushroom soup

tortilla chips

Combine beef and sausage in a heavy large saucepan over low heat; add cheese. Heat until cheese is melted; mix in soup, stirring until warmed through. Serve with chips.

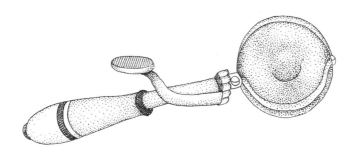

Use a cookie scoop to shape meatballs...so simple!

Cranberry Meatballs

Serves 6 to 8

16-oz. can jellied cranberry
    sauce
12-oz. bottle chili sauce
1/2 c. brown sugar, packed
1 T. lemon juice
2 lbs. ground beef
1 t. dried parsley
2 T. soy sauce

1/2 t. garlic salt
2 T. onion
1 c. quick-cooking oats,
    uncooked
2 eggs, beaten
1/4 t. pepper
1/3 c. catsup

Mix together first 4 ingredients; set aside. Combine remaining ingredients in a large bowl. Form into 2-inch balls; arrange in a shallow ungreased roasting pan. Spoon cranberry mixture over top. Bake at 350 degrees for 40 to 50 minutes.

For a new twist, substitute packaged stuffing mix for
bread crumbs in meatball or meatloaf recipes.

Sauerkraut Balls

Makes 4 to 5 dozen

1/3 c. onion, chopped
1 c. margarine
2 c. all-purpose flour, divided
2-1/2 c. milk, divided
2 lbs. ground beef, browned and
    drained
1 T. prepared horseradish
1 t. Worcestershire sauce

1-1/2 t. dry mustard
2 drops hot pepper sauce
salt and pepper to taste
16-oz. can sauerkraut, drained
1 egg, beaten
1 c. bread crumbs
oil for deep frying

Sauté onion in margarine over medium heat. Stir in one cup flour; cook for one minute and blend in 1-1/2 cups milk. Cook for an additional minute, stirring constantly. Remove from heat; set aside. Combine beef, horseradish, Worcestershire sauce, mustard, hot pepper sauce, salt and pepper; cook for 3 minutes. Remove from heat; mix in sauerkraut. Pour in milk mixture; stir and chill for at least 4 hours, or overnight. Shape into walnut-size balls; roll in remaining flour. Combine egg and remaining milk. Dip balls in egg mixture; coat with bread crumbs. Deep-fry in 375-degree oil until done. Drain on paper towels.

It's amazing how much the little niceties of life
have to do with making dinner pleasant.
-Book of Etiquette by Lillian Eichler, 1921

BBQ Beef Cups

Serves 10

3/4 lb. ground beef, browned
   and drained
1/2 c. barbecue sauce
1 T. dried, minced onion

2 T. brown sugar, packed
12-oz. tube refrigerated biscuits
3/4 c. shredded Cheddar cheese

Combine ground beef, sauce, onion, and brown sugar; mix well and set aside. Separate and press biscuit dough into ungreased muffin cups; divide mixture evenly into cups. Sprinkle with cheese. Bake at 400 degrees for 10 to 12 minutes.

Pick up a dozen pint-size Mason jars...perfect for serving
cold beverages at casual get-togethers.

Hearty Cheeseburger Bread

Serves 8 to 10

2 lbs. ground beef, browned and
    drained
1/2 t. garlic powder
1/4 c. butter, softened
1 loaf French bread, cut in half
    horizontally

16-oz. container sour cream
12-oz. pkg. shredded Cheddar
    cheese

Combine beef and garlic powder; set aside. Spread butter on both
halves of bread; place on an ungreased baking sheet. Stir sour
cream into beef mixture; spread onto bread. Sprinkle with cheese.
Bake at 350 degrees for 15 to 20 minutes, until cheese is melted;
slice to serve.

Make fancy cheese curls for garnishing servings of
Deep-Dish Taco Squares...simply pull a vegetable peeler
across a block of cheese.

Deep-Dish Taco Squares

Serves 12 to 15

2 c. biscuit baking mix
1/2 c. water
1 lb. ground beef
1 green pepper, chopped
1 onion, chopped
1/8 t. garlic powder
8-oz. can tomato sauce
1-1/4 oz. pkg. taco seasoning
  mix

1 c. shredded Cheddar cheese
8-oz. container sour cream
1/3 c. mayonnaise-type salad
  dressing
1/4 t. paprika
Garnish: sour cream, chopped
  tomatoes, chopped lettuce,
  chopped onion

Combine baking mix and water; spread in a greased 13"x9" baking pan. Bake at 375 degrees for 9 minutes; remove from oven and set aside. Brown ground beef with green pepper, onion and garlic powder; drain. Stir in tomato sauce and taco seasoning; spread over crust. Combine cheese, sour cream and salad dressing; spoon over beef mixture. Sprinkle with paprika. Bake, uncovered, at 375 degrees for an additional 25 minutes. Cut into squares; garnish as desired.

Why not get out Mom's soup tureen set for cozy soup dinners? The ladle makes serving easy and the lid keeps soup piping hot and steamy.

Santa Fe Cheese Soup

1 lb. ground beef
1 onion, chopped
15-oz. can ranch-style beans
14-1/2 oz. can diced tomatoes

15-1/4 oz. can corn, drained
16-oz. pkg. pasteurized process
   cheese spread, cubed

In a stockpot, cook ground beef and onion over medium heat until beef is browned; drain. Stir in remaining ingredients. Simmer for 15 to 20 minutes, until cheese is melted.

Heaven is a pot of chili simmering on the stove.
-Charles Simic

Chilly Weather Chili

1 lb. ground beef
2 T. onion, diced
15-3/4 oz. can chili beans with chili sauce
8-1/4 oz. can refried beans

8-oz. can tomato sauce
8-oz. jar salsa
1/2 c. water
Garnish: shredded Cheddar cheese, sour cream

Brown beef and onion together in a large stockpot over medium heat; drain. Add remaining ingredients except garnish. Bring to a boil and reduce heat to medium; cover and simmer for 30 minutes, stirring occasionally. Garnish as desired.

Save chopping time...use a garlic press. Don't even bother peeling the clove, just place it in the garlic press and close. The peel slides right off and the paste is easily removed for any recipe.

Stuffed Green Pepper Soup

Serves 6

1-1/2 lbs. ground beef
1 onion, chopped
3 cloves garlic, minced
1 green pepper, chopped
3 14-1/2 oz. cans stewed
   tomatoes

2 8-oz. cans tomato sauce
6-oz. pkg. white or brown rice,
   cooked

Brown ground beef, onion and garlic together until beef is no longer pink; drain. Add green pepper and tomatoes with juice; cook until pepper is tender. Add tomato sauce and simmer for 15 minutes. Add rice and simmer until heated through. Makes 6 servings.

Need to thicken a kettle of soup?
Just stir in a little quick-cooking oats.

Italian Wedding Soup

Serves 10

1 lb. ground beef
1 lb. ground sausage
4 eggs, divided and beaten
1 c. soft bread crumbs
2 t. dried oregano
1 t. dried rosemary
1 clove garlic, pressed
1 to 2 T. olive oil
2 14-oz. cans chicken broth

3-2/3 c. water
5-oz. pkg. vermicelli pasta,
  uncooked
1 c. spinach, torn
1 onion, thinly sliced
6 mushrooms, thinly sliced
Garnish: grated Parmesan
  cheese

Combine beef, sausage, 2 beaten eggs and next 4 ingredients in a
large bowl. Shape mixture into bite-size meatballs. Heat olive oil in
a large skillet over medium heat. Gently brown meatballs until
cooked; drain and set aside. In a large stockpot, combine broth and
water; bring to a boil over medium-high heat. Add pasta, meatballs,
spinach, onion and mushrooms. Simmer, uncovered, until tender. Stir
in remaining eggs, stirring only until eggs are set. Ladle into
bowls and garnish with cheese.

Slip sparkly bangle bracelets around rolled dinner napkins
for playful table settings!

Martin's Marvelous Minestrone

Serves 4 to 6

1 lb. ground beef
1 onion, chopped
1 c. potatoes, peeled and
    chopped
1 c. carrots, peeled and chopped
1/2 c. celery, diced
28-oz. can diced tomatoes
4 c. water
1 bay leaf

1/2 t. dried thyme
1/4 t. dried basil
1 to 2 t. salt
1/8 t. pepper
1/4 c. long-cooking rice,
    uncooked
Garnish: grated Parmesan
    cheese

Brown ground beef and onion in a stockpot over medium heat; drain. Add potatoes, carrots, celery, tomatoes and water. Bring to a boil; add seasonings. Reduce heat; cover and simmer for 30 minutes. Add rice and cook for an additional 30 minutes, or until rice is tender. Discard bay leaf. Ladle into soup bowls and sprinkle with cheese.

It's so easy to freshen up yesterday's crusty rolls to enjoy with today's soup. Simply sprinkle with water and bake at 400 degrees for 6 to 8 minutes.

Beef-Vegetable Soup

Serves 6 to 8

1 lb. ground beef
1 T. dried, minced onion
1 t. garlic, minced
28-oz. can diced tomatoes
6 c. water
2 T. lemon juice
2 T. balsamic vinegar

4 cubes beef bouillon
1 c. corn
1 c. carrots, peeled and chopped
1 c. peas
salt and pepper to taste
1/2 c. orzo pasta, uncooked

Brown beef, onion and garlic in a large stockpot over medium heat; drain. Stir in remaining ingredients and simmer over medium heat for 30 minutes.

Happy is...the family which can eat onions together.
-Charles Dudley Warner

Hearty Cabbage Stew

Serves 4 to 6

1 lb. ground beef
1 onion, chopped
1 T. chili powder
1 head cabbage, chopped
2 stalks celery, chopped
1 green pepper, chopped
15-1/4 oz. can corn, drained
14-1/2 oz. can tomatoes with
    green chiles

14-1/2 oz. can diced tomatoes
14-1/2 oz. can sliced carrots,
    drained
15-oz. can ranch-style beans
8-oz. can tomato sauce
1 t. garlic salt
1 t. salt
1 t. pepper

Brown ground beef, onion and chili powder over medium heat in a stockpot; drain. Add remaining ingredients; reduce heat and simmer for 45 minutes to one hour.

Pour olive oil into saucers and sprinkle with a little Italian seasoning...perfect for dipping slices of warm crusty bread.

Slow-Cooker Pizza Stew

Serves 6 to 8

1-1/2 lbs. ground beef
1 onion, chopped
2 10-oz. cans pizza sauce
10-oz. jar sliced mushrooms,
    drained

16-oz. pkg. shredded
    mozzarella cheese
10-oz. pkg. sliced pepperoni
8-oz. pkg. rotini pasta, cooked

Brown ground beef and onion in a large skillet over medium heat;
drain. Add pizza sauce and mushrooms, heating through. Layer beef
mixture, cheese and pepperoni in a slow cooker; cover and cook on
low setting for 8 hours. Toss with cooked rotini before serving.

A round, clear glass fish bowl makes a delightful centerpiece, filled
with colored sand and seashells or shiny ornament balls.

Easy Taco Soup

Serves 6 to 8

1 lb. ground beef
1 onion, chopped
1-1/2 c. water
15-1/4 oz. can corn, drained
3 15-1/2 oz. cans Mexican chili
    beans
15-oz. can tomato sauce

14-1/2 oz. can diced tomatoes
4-oz. can chopped green chiles
1-1/4 oz. pkg. taco seasoning
    mix
Garnish: shredded lettuce,
    chopped tomato, shredded
    Cheddar cheese, sour cream

Brown ground beef and onion in a Dutch oven over medium heat.
Cook until beef is browned and onion is tender, stirring to break up
meat; drain. Stir in remaining ingredients except garnish; bring to a
boil. Reduce heat and simmer, uncovered, for 15 minutes, stirring
occasionally. Ladle soup into bowls; garnish as desired.

Turn plain kitchen towels into something special...simply
stitch on embroidered trim.

Black Bean Chili

Serves 4 to 6

1 lb. dried black beans
1 lb. ground beef
1 onion, chopped
3 cloves garlic, minced
3 T. chili powder

2 T. oil
1 T. cumin seed
1 T. Worcestershire sauce
28-oz. can puréed tomatoes
1 green pepper, chopped

Place beans in a stockpot, cover with water and soak overnight.
Drain water and cover beans with fresh water. Simmer over low
heat until tender, about 2 hours. In a large skillet over medium heat,
brown ground beef, onion, garlic and chili powder in oil until beef is
no longer pink. Stir into beans; add remaining ingredients. Simmer
over medium-low heat for one hour, until beans are very tender.

A pottery pitcher makes handy storage for ladles, wooden spoons, spatulas and other cooking tools.

Mexican Meatball Soup

Serves 6 to 8

3/4 lb. ground beef
3/4 lb. ground pork
1/3 c. instant rice, uncooked
1-1/2 t. salt
1/4 t. pepper
1 egg, beaten

1 T. fresh mint, minced
1 onion, minced
1 clove garlic, minced
1 T. oil
10-3/4 oz. can tomato soup
3 qts. beef broth

Mix together beef, pork, rice, salt, pepper, egg and mint; shape into one-inch balls and set aside. In a large stockpot, sauté onion and garlic in oil over medium heat; drain. Add tomato soup and broth. Heat until boiling; place meatballs into broth. Cover and simmer for 30 minutes, until meatballs are cooked through.

Fill up a big party tray with fresh veggies as a handy
side dish for sandwiches. Any extras can be tossed into
a crunchy salad the next day.

Uncle Joe's Sloppy Joes

Serves 6 to 8

2 lbs. ground beef
1 onion, chopped
1/2 c. green pepper, chopped
1/2 c. celery, chopped
2 14-1/2 oz. cans stewed
   tomatoes
2 c. tomato sauce

1/2 c. catsup
1/4 c. brown sugar, packed
2 T. spicy mustard
1 T. Worcestershire sauce
1/4 t. salt
1/4 t. pepper
6 to 8 sandwich buns, split

Brown ground beef, onion, green pepper and celery in a large skillet over medium heat; drain. Add remaining ingredients except buns. Bring to a boil; reduce heat and simmer for one hour, stirring occasionally. Spoon onto buns and serve.

Burgers don't have to be ordinary...try making them with
ground turkey, chicken or even ground sausage. Season them
with Italian, Mexican, Thai, Southwest or Mediterranean blends
easily found at the meat counter.

Tavern Burgers

Serves 4

1 T. oil
1 lb. ground beef
1 c. chicken broth
1 t. paprika
1 t. Worcestershire sauce

salt and pepper to taste
2 t. mustard
4 hamburger buns, split
1/2 c. onion, finely chopped
1 dill pickle, sliced

Heat oil in a skillet over medium heat. Add ground beef, breaking apart as it browns; drain. Add chicken broth, paprika, Worcestershire sauce, salt and pepper; bring to a boil. Reduce heat to medium-low; simmer for 15 minutes, stirring occasionally. Spread 1/2 teaspoon mustard on top half of each bun; set aside. Spoon ground beef mixture evenly among 4 buns; top with onion, dill pickle and top half of bun.

Pour hot tea into ice cube trays, drop in mini lemon wedges, then freeze. They'll keep iced tea cold without watering it down.

48

Aloha Burgers

Serves 4

8-oz. can pineapple slices,
    drained and juice reserved
3/4 c. teriyaki sauce
1 lb. ground beef
1 T. butter, softened

4 hamburger buns, split
4 slices Swiss cheese
4 slices bacon, crisply cooked
4 lettuce leaves
1 red onion, sliced

Stir together reserved pineapple juice and teriyaki sauce in a small bowl. Place pineapple slices and 3 tablespoons juice mixture into a plastic zipping bag. Turn to coat; set aside. Shape ground beef into 4 patties and spoon remaining juice mixture over top; set aside. Spread butter on buns; set aside. Grill patties over medium-high heat to desired doneness, turning to cook on both sides. Place buns on grill, cut-side down, to toast lightly. Remove pineapple slices from plastic bag; place on grill and heat through until lightly golden, about one minute per side. Serve burgers on buns topped with pineapple, cheese, bacon, lettuce and onion.

Just for fun, turn vintage heat-resistant jelly glasses into candles. Holding a wick in place, pour scented wax gel into each glass...so easy!

Beefy Filled Hard Rolls

Makes 12

2 lbs. ground beef
1/4 c. onion, diced
10-3/4 oz. can cream of
    mushroom soup

1/2 c. shredded Colby cheese
salt and pepper to taste
12 small French hard rolls,
    sliced and hollowed out

Brown ground beef with onion in a skillet over medium heat; drain. Add soup and simmer for 5 minutes. Stir in cheese, salt and pepper; cook until cheese melts. Fill rolls with meat mixture and top with top halves of rolls.

Bakery-fresh bread...easy! Thaw frozen dough, roll out and sprinkle with minced garlic and chopped rosemary. Roll up and bake as the package directs.

Hearty Italian Sandwiches

1 lb. ground beef
1 lb. ground Italian pork
    sausage
1 onion, chopped
1 green pepper, chopped
1 red pepper, chopped

1 t. salt
1 t. pepper
1/2 t. red pepper flakes
3/4 c. Italian salad dressing
12 sandwich rolls, split
12 slices provolone cheese

Brown ground beef and sausage together in a skillet; drain and set aside. Place one-third of onion and peppers in a slow cooker; top with half of meat mixture. Repeat layers with remaining vegetables and meat. Sprinkle with salt, pepper and red pepper flakes; pour salad dressing over top. Cover and cook on low setting for 6 hours. Serve on rolls, topped with cheese.

Decorate plain paper cups with ribbons, bows, stickers and flowers...anything but plain!

Pizza Burgers

Makes 2 dozen

2 lbs. ground beef
1/2 green pepper, diced
1 onion, diced
2 T. sugar
26-oz. can spaghetti sauce
  with mushrooms

6-oz. can tomato paste
1 doz. hamburger buns, split
8-oz. pkg. shredded mozzarella
  cheese
1/2 c. grated Parmesan cheese

Brown ground beef with pepper, onion and sugar in a skillet; drain and set aside. Mix spaghetti sauce with tomato paste; stir into beef mixture. Spread on each bun; sprinkle with cheeses. Arrange on ungreased baking sheets. Bake at 500 degrees for 5 minutes, until cheese melts.

Box lunches are a great way to serve up special dinners.
Shoe boxes are charming when covered with wallpaper scraps
and topped with ribbons and bows.

Tex-Mex Meatball Subs

Makes 8

1-1/2 lbs. ground beef
1 egg, beaten
1 c. tortilla chips, crushed
16-oz. jar salsa, divided
26-oz. jar spaghetti sauce

8 hoagie or sub buns, split
1 c. shredded Monterey Jack
   cheese
Optional: sliced jalapeño
   peppers

Mix together ground beef, egg, chips and one cup salsa. Form mixture into one-inch balls; place in an ungreased 13"x9" baking pan. Bake at 375 degrees for 45 minutes; remove from oven and drain. Combine spaghetti sauce and remaining salsa in a saucepan; heat through and pour over meatballs. Spoon meatballs onto buns and top with cheese. Garnish with jalapeño peppers, if desired.

Keep it simple...wrap dinnerware in napkins and tie up
with colorful ribbons.

Super Scrumptious Soft Tacos

Makes 8

1 lb. ground beef
2/3 c. water
1 T. chili powder
1/2 t. salt
1/4 t. garlic powder
1/4 t. cayenne pepper
15-1/2 oz. can kidney beans,
    drained and rinsed

1 head lettuce, torn
1 c. shredded Cheddar cheese
2/3 c. sliced black olives
2 tomatoes, chopped
1 onion, chopped
8 10-inch flour tortillas
Garnish: chopped avocado,
    sour cream

Brown ground beef in a large skillet, stirring occasionally; drain. Stir in water, chili powder, salt, garlic powder, cayenne pepper and beans. Heat to boiling; reduce heat and simmer for 15 minutes, stirring occasionally. Remove from heat; set aside to cool for 10 minutes. Toss lettuce, cheese, olives, tomatoes and onion in a large bowl. Spoon beef mixture down the centers of tortillas; sprinkle with lettuce mixture. Garnish with avocado and sour cream.

Having a picnic or grilling out on a breezy day? Cast-off clip earrings make sparkly tablecloth weights...simply clip 'em to the 4 corners of the cloth.

Grilled Garlic Burgers

Makes 4

1-3/4 lbs. ground beef
2 T. garlic, minced
1/2 c. onion, finely chopped
1 t. salt
1 t. pepper
1 to 2 T. prepared horseradish

1 T. oil
2 T. mustard
1/2 c. plus 2 T. catsup
2 T. sour cream
4 onion buns, split and grilled

In a mixing bowl, mix together ground beef, garlic, onion, salt and pepper. Shape into 4 patties. Spread with horseradish and press into meat. Coat grill or a large skillet with oil and cook burgers for 4 to 5 minutes per side. While cooking, mix together mustard, catsup and sour cream. Top burgers with catsup mixture and serve on grilled buns.

Colorful straws layered with slices of kiwi, banana and pineapple are
fun fruit skewers for glasses of ice water or frosty lemonade.

Yummy Blue Cheese Burgers

2 lbs. ground beef
Cajun seasoning to taste
1 c. half-and-half
1 clove garlic, finely minced
1 t. dried rosemary
1 t. dried basil

4-oz. container crumbled
  blue cheese
6 kaiser rolls, split, toasted
  and buttered
Optional: sliced mushrooms,
  sliced onion, butter

Shape ground beef into 6 patties; sprinkle with Cajun seasoning to taste. Grill to desired doneness; set aside and keep warm. Combine half-and-half, garlic and herbs in a saucepan; simmer over low heat until thickened and reduced by half. Add blue cheese and stir just until melted. Place burgers on rolls; spoon sauce over burgers. If desired, sauté mushrooms and onion in butter until tender; spoon onto burgers.

Let everyone at the next potluck know what's inside your casserole dish. Glue a beribboned fresh herb sprig to a mailing tag, write the casserole name on the tag and tie onto the lid knob.

Spinach-Mushroom Bake

Serves 6

2 7-1/2 oz. tubes refrigerated
   buttermilk biscuits
1-1/2 lbs. ground beef
1/2 c. onion, finely chopped
2 eggs, beaten
10-oz. pkg. frozen chopped
   spinach, thawed and
   drained

4-oz. can sliced mushrooms,
   drained
1 c. shredded Monterey Jack
   cheese
1/4 c. grated Parmesan cheese
1-1/2 t. garlic powder
salt and pepper to taste
1 to 2 T. butter, melted

Flatten biscuits and press into a lightly greased 11"x7" baking pan;
set aside. Brown ground beef with onion; drain and set aside. Blend
together eggs, spinach and mushrooms. Add cheeses, garlic powder,
salt, pepper and beef mixture. Spoon over biscuits; drizzle with butter.
Bake, uncovered, at 375 degrees for 25 to 30 minutes, until golden.

Find a jumbo-size dish for serving up pasta-filled
casseroles...makes helping yourself so much easier.

Cheddar Ziti Bake

Serves 8

1 lb. sweet Italian pork sausage
    links
1 lb. ground beef
1 onion, chopped
2 29-oz. cans crushed tomatoes

1 c. red wine or beef broth
1 T. Italian seasoning
16-oz. pkg. ziti pasta, cooked
16-oz. pkg. shredded Cheddar
    cheese

Place sausages in a saucepan; cover with water. Boil for 15 to
20 minutes; drain and rinse under cold water. Cut into 1/2-inch slices;
brown with ground beef in a large skillet over medium heat. Add
onion and sauté until tender; drain. Add tomatoes and wine or broth;
stir in seasoning. Heat until boiling; reduce heat and simmer until
thickened. Remove from heat; pour 1/4 cup sauce into an ungreased
roasting pan. Add half the pasta, half the remaining sauce and half
the cheese; repeat layers. Bake, uncovered, at 325 degrees until
bubbly, about 40 minutes.

To keep a bouquet of pretty blossoms fresh, add a spoonful of sugar and a little lemon-lime soda to the water.

Topsy-Turvy Lasagna

Serves 6 to 8

3/4 lb. ground beef
28-oz. jar spaghetti sauce
5 c. cooked wide egg noodles

1 c. cottage cheese
8-oz. pkg. shredded mozzarella
   cheese, divided

Brown ground beef in a skillet over medium heat; drain. Stir in spaghetti sauce; simmer for 10 minutes. In a lightly greased 2-quart casserole dish, combine noodles, ground beef mixture, cottage cheese and one cup mozzarella cheese. Top with remaining mozzarella. Bake, uncovered, at 350 degrees for 15 to 20 minutes.

Mini choppers make prep work a breeze for chopping onions,
potatoes or celery...what a time saver!

Dinner in a Pinch

Serves 4

1 lb. ground beef, browned and
    drained
1/4 c. onion, chopped
1 stalk celery, sliced
2 potatoes, peeled and sliced

14-1/2 oz. can tomatoes with
    chiles
14-1/2 oz. can green beans,
    drained
salt and pepper to taste

Combine all ingredients in a large skillet over medium heat; stir gently.
Simmer until potatoes are tender, about 20 minutes.

Clever placecards...rubber stamp names on twill tape, tie around a rolled-up napkin and place in the center of each plate.

Cornbread-Topped Beef Bake

Serves 6

1/2 lb. ground beef
1 onion, chopped
3 slices bacon, crisply cooked,
    crumbled and drippings
    reserved
10-3/4 oz. can tomato soup
2/3 c. water
2 16-oz. cans black beans,
    drained and rinsed

1 t. chili powder
1/2 t. garlic powder
Optional: 1/4 t. red pepper
    flakes
1 c. shredded Cheddar cheese
8-1/2 oz. pkg. cornbread mix

Brown beef and onion in reserved drippings over medium heat; drain. Stir in soup, water, bacon, beans and seasonings. Simmer over low heat for 20 minutes, stirring often and adding a little more water if necessary. Sprinkle cheese over beef mixture; mix well. Pour into a lightly greased 13"x9" baking pan; set aside. Prepare cornbread batter according to package directions; spread over beef mixture. Bake, uncovered, at 400 degrees for 20 to 30 minutes, until cornbread is golden.

If you're planning to garnish servings with tomatoes, keep the tomatoes stored at room temperature for the best fresh-from-the-garden taste.

Enchilada Casserole

Serves 6 to 8

1-1/2 lbs. ground beef, browned and drained
14-oz. can enchilada sauce
10-3/4 oz. can cream of mushroom soup

10-3/4 oz. can cream of chicken soup
10 6-inch corn tortillas, torn
8-oz. pkg. shredded Cheddar cheese

Combine ground beef, sauce and soups in a large bowl. Stir until well mixed. In a greased 13"x9" baking pan, layer half each of the tortillas, meat mixture and cheese. Repeat layers. Bake, uncovered, at 350 degrees for 30 minutes.

When toting Southwestern Casserole to a potluck, tie a colorful bandanna around the casserole dish and slip a wooden spoon inside the knot. A clever way to wrap it all up!

Southwestern Casserole

2 lbs. ground beef
1 onion, chopped
2 8-oz. cans enchilada sauce
2 15-oz. cans chili beans with
  sauce

13-1/2 oz. pkg. tortilla chips,
  divided
8-oz. pkg. shredded Cheddar
  cheese
Garnish: sour cream

Brown beef and onion together in a skillet over medium heat; drain.
Stir in enchilada sauce and beans. Coarsely break up tortilla chips,
reserving 1/2 cup. Arrange remaining chips in a lightly greased
13"x9" baking pan; spread meat mixture on top. Sprinkle with
reserved tortilla chips and Cheddar cheese. Bake, covered, at
350 degrees for 30 minutes. Remove from oven; garnish with sour
cream. Serve immediately.

When serving bread with casseroles, vintage
tea towels are perfect bread basket liners and
add a splash of color to any table.

Hamburger-Noodle Bake

Serves 8

1 lb. ground beef
1/2 c. onion, chopped
2 8-oz. cans tomato sauce
1 T. sugar
3/4 t. garlic salt
1/4 t. pepper

4 c. cooked medium egg noodles
1 c. cottage cheese
1/4 c. sour cream
8-oz. pkg. cream cheese,
    softened
1/4 c. grated Parmesan cheese

Brown ground beef and onion together; drain. Stir in tomato sauce,
sugar, garlic salt and pepper; heat through and remove from heat.
Gently combine noodles, cottage cheese, sour cream and cream
cheese; spread half the mixture in a lightly greased 11"x7" baking
pan. Cover with half the meat mixture; repeat layers. Sprinkle with
Parmesan cheese. Bake, covered, at 350 degrees for 30 minutes.

Line the casserole dish with aluminum foil whenever you
plan to freeze a casserole...clean-up will be a snap!

Stuffed Cabbage Casserole

Serves 6 to 8

10 c. cabbage, chopped and
    divided
2 lbs. ground beef
1/2 c. instant rice, uncooked
1 t. salt
1 t. garlic powder

3/4 c. sour cream
1 onion, chopped
2 10-3/4 oz. cans tomato soup
1/2 c. catsup
1 c. shredded Colby cheese

Place half the cabbage in a greased 13"x9" baking pan; set aside. Combine ground beef, rice, salt, garlic powder, sour cream and onion; spread over cabbage. Layer remaining cabbage over meat mixture; top with tomato soup, then catsup. Sprinkle with cheese. Bake, covered, at 350 degrees for 2 hours, until hot and bubbly.

Look for old restaurant serving dishes at flea markets and antique shops...they're roomy enough to hold the largest family recipes.

Pepperoni Pasta Casserole

Serves 24

2 lbs. ground beef
1 onion, chopped
2 28-oz. jars spaghetti sauce
16-oz. pkg. rotini pasta, cooked

16-oz. pkg. shredded
   mozzarella cheese, divided
8-oz. pkg. sliced pepperoni,
   divided

Brown ground beef with onion; drain. Stir in spaghetti sauce and pasta; spread equally in 2 greased 13"x9" baking pans. Sprinkle cheese over both pans; arrange pepperoni slices on top. Bake at 350 degrees for 25 to 30 minutes.

Dress up Nacho Grande Casserole with green onion starbursts. Cut the green tops into long, thin slices. Soak in ice water for 15 minutes and they'll curl open.

Nacho Grande Casserole

Serves 8 to 10

2 lbs. ground beef
1 onion, chopped
15-oz. can tomato sauce
2 16-oz. cans spicy chili beans
1-1/4 oz. pkg. taco seasoning
   mix
16-oz. pkg. frozen corn, thawed
8-oz. pkg. finely shredded
   Cheddar Jack cheese,
   divided

9-oz. pkg. nacho-flavored
   tortilla chips, crushed and
   divided
Optional: sour cream, chopped
   tomato, chopped green
   onion

Brown ground beef and onion in a Dutch oven; drain. Add tomato
sauce, beans, seasoning mix and corn; stir until blended. Simmer over
medium heat for 10 minutes. Pour half of beef mixture into a greased
13"x9" baking pan. Top with half each of the cheese and crushed
chips; repeat layers. Bake at 350 degrees for 25 to 30 minutes, until
bubbly and golden. Top portions with a dollop of sour cream and
a sprinkling of tomato and green onion, if desired.

Stack 2 cake plates for serving a variety of dinner rolls in style.

Cheddar Barbecue

Serves 6

1-1/2 lbs. ground beef
1 c. onion, chopped
16-oz. can barbecue-style beans
10-3/4 oz. can tomato soup
1 t. chili powder

1/2 t. salt
1/2 t. paprika
1/4 t. garlic salt
12-oz. tube refrigerated biscuits
1 c. shredded Cheddar cheese

Brown ground beef and onion together; drain. Add beans, soup and seasonings; bring to a boil. Spread mixture into a greased 2-quart casserole dish. Arrange biscuits on top of mixture; sprinkle with cheese. Bake at 375 degrees for 25 to 30 minutes.

Salads are perfect paired with any main dish, so plant lots of leaf lettuce in your garden. Just trim off what you need and the plant will continue to grow and give you crispy lettuce all summer.

Cheese-Stuffed Meatloaf

Serves 4 to 6

1-1/2 lbs. ground beef
15-oz. can spaghetti sauce,
    divided
2 eggs, beaten
1 c. bread crumbs
1/4 c. onion, chopped

1-1/2 T. dried parsley
1 t. salt
1/4 t. pepper
1-1/2 c. shredded mozzarella
    cheese, divided

Combine ground beef, one cup sauce and remaining ingredients except cheese; mix well. Divide meat mixture into thirds; spread one-third in an ungreased 9"x5" loaf pan. Sprinkle half the cheese over top. Repeat layers, ending with meat. Bake, uncovered, at 350 degrees for 30 minutes. Spread remaining sauce over top. Bake, uncovered, for an additional 30 minutes.

Packages of prepared mashed potatoes from your grocer are a quick & easy way to top Shepherd's Pie... homemade taste without the work!

90

Shepherd's Pie

Serves 6 to 8

1 lb. ground beef
1 T. oil
1 clove garlic, chopped
2 shallots, sliced
1 onion, chopped
1 t. salt
1 t. pepper
2 T. all-purpose flour

1 c. beef broth
1 T. tomato paste
1 c. frozen peas, thawed
2 T. fresh parsley, chopped
4 c. mashed potatoes
1 c. shredded Cheddar cheese
1/4 c. grated Parmesan cheese

Brown beef in oil with garlic, shallots and onion; drain. Add salt, pepper and flour; cook for 3 to 4 minutes over medium heat. Add beef broth and tomato paste, stirring until mixture becomes creamy. Add peas and parsley, heating through. Pour mixture into an ungreased 13"x9" baking pan. Spread mashed potatoes over top; sprinkle with cheeses. Bake, uncovered, at 400 degrees for 20 minutes, until golden.

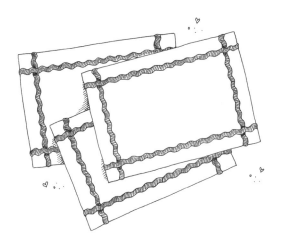

For a quick-to-stitch placemat, transform plain placemats
with a trim of rick rack.

Mom's Meatloaf

Serves 4 to 6

1 lb. ground beef
1 egg, beaten
1/3 c. bread crumbs
1/2 c. milk
1 t. salt

1 onion, diced
1/4 c. catsup
3 T. brown sugar, packed
1/4 t. nutmeg
1 t. dry mustard

Mix together beef, egg, bread crumbs, milk, salt and onion; spread in an ungreased 9"x5" loaf pan. Combine remaining ingredients; spread on top. Bake, uncovered, at 350 degrees for one hour.

Fluffy baked potatoes for a crowd... just fix & forget! Pierce
10 to 12 baking potatoes with a fork and wrap each in aluminum foil.
Arrange potatoes in a slow cooker, cover and cook on high setting
for 2-1/2 to 4 hours, until fork tender.

Bacon-Mushroom Spaghetti Pie

Serves 4 to 6

1/2 lb. ground beef
1/2 c. onion, chopped
8-oz. can sliced mushrooms,
    drained
14-1/2 oz. can diced tomatoes
10-3/4 oz. can tomato soup
1/2 t. pepper

1/2 t. dried, minced garlic
8-oz. pkg. shredded Cheddar
    cheese, divided
8-oz. pkg. spaghetti, cooked
4 slices bacon, crisply cooked
    and crumbled

Brown ground beef, onion and mushrooms in a large skillet over
medium heat, stirring occasionally; drain. Reduce heat; stir in
tomatoes, soup, pepper and garlic. Add 1-1/2 cups cheese, stirring
until melted. Add spaghetti and bacon; toss to combine. Pour into a
greased 2-quart casserole dish. Bake, covered, at 350 degrees for
30 minutes, or until bubbly and heated through. Uncover; sprinkle
with remaining cheese. Let stand for 5 to 10 minutes, until cheese
is melted.

A can't-go-wrong mix of vintage and new tableware is always a fun and different way to serve up dinner.

Flaky Beef Pie

1 lb. ground beef
1 onion, chopped
1 clove garlic, minced
8-oz. can tomato sauce
4-oz. can sliced mushrooms,
    drained

1 t. salt
1 t. chili powder
2 9-inch pie crusts

Brown beef, onion and garlic in a large skillet; drain. Add tomato
sauce, mushrooms, salt and chili powder; heat through. Line an
ungreased 9" round cake pan with one crust; fill with beef mixture.
Cover pie with remaining crust; crimp and seal edges. Cut several
vents. Bake at 425 degrees for 20 to 25 minutes, until crust is golden.

Keep the week's running menu at a glance. Tack
extra-wide rick rack to a bulletin board and just slip your
grocery list underneath.

Mexicali Pie

Serves 6 to 8

1 lb. ground beef
1/2 c. onion, chopped
1/2 c. green pepper, chopped
1-1/2 c. frozen corn, thawed
   and drained

1 c. chunky salsa
3/4 c. shredded Cheddar cheese
1/8 t. pepper
1 c. corn chips, crushed

Brown ground beef, onion and pepper in a skillet; drain. Add corn, salsa, Cheddar cheese and pepper. Spoon into a lightly greased 10" pie plate; top with crushed chips. Bake at 350 degrees for 30 minutes; let cool for 10 minutes.

Serve crisp salads in hollowed-out oranges, avocados
or tomatoes for a tasty change.

Meatloaf Pie

Serves 6

2 lbs. ground beef
1 onion, chopped
1 green pepper, chopped
1/2 c. catsup
1 t. mustard
1/2 c. quick-cooking oats,
    uncooked

1 c. Italian-seasoned bread
    crumbs
1 egg, beaten
1/4 c. water
1 t. Worcestershire sauce
4 slices American cheese

Combine all ingredients except cheese; spoon into an ungreased
9" deep-dish pie plate. Bake at 350 degrees for one hour. Cut each
slice of cheese diagonally in half to form 8 triangles; arrange on top of
pie. Return to oven for 3 to 4 minutes, until cheese melts.

Cranberries not only make mini Cranberry Meatloaves taste extra
special, they're great added to a tossed salad. They give salads a
terrific sweet-tart taste.

Cranberry Meatloaves

Serves 5

1 lb. ground beef
1 c. cooked rice
1/2 c. tomato juice
1 egg, beaten
1/4 c. onion, minced

1 t. salt
16-oz. can whole-berry
  cranberry sauce
1/3 c. brown sugar, packed
1 T. lemon juice

Combine beef, rice, tomato juice, egg, onion and salt. Shape into
5 mini meatloaves and place in an ungreased 13"x9" baking pan. In a
small bowl, mix together cranberry sauce, brown sugar and lemon
juice; spoon over top of each loaf. Bake at 350 degrees for 45 minutes.

Float lemon and lime slices along with a few sliced strawberries in a pitcher of icy water to make it taste anything but ordinary!

Beefy Onion Bake

Serves 8

1 lb. ground beef, browned
10-3/4 oz. can cream of
    mushroom soup
10-3/4 oz. can cream of
    celery soup
10-3/4 oz. can cream of
    chicken soup

1-1/2 oz. pkg. dry onion
    soup mix
2 c. instant rice, uncooked
1-1/2 c. water

Combine ingredients together; spread in an ungreased 13"x9" baking pan. Bake at 325 degrees for 45 minutes.

Make dinner invitations fun! Gather pretty posies, tie on
an invitation tag and deliver to friends.

Salisbury Steak & Onion Gravy

Serves 6

10-1/2 oz. can French onion
   soup, divided
1-1/2 lbs. ground beef
1/2 c. bread crumbs
1 egg, beaten
1/4 t. salt

1/8 t. pepper
1 T. all-purpose flour
1/4 c. catsup
1/4 c. water
1 t. Worcestershire sauce
1/2 t. mustard

Combine 1/2 cup soup, beef, bread crumbs, egg, salt and pepper in a
large mixing bowl; shape into 6 patties. Brown in a skillet over
medium heat; drain and set aside. Gradually blend remaining soup
with flour until smooth; add remaining ingredients. Pour into skillet;
stir well. Cover; return to heat and simmer for 20 minutes,
stirring occasionally.

Vintage-style souvenir tea towels make whimsical
oversized napkins...so handy!

Chinese Beef & Noodles

Serves 4 to 6

1-1/4 lbs. ground beef
2 3-oz. pkgs. Oriental-flavored
     ramen noodles, crushed,
     with seasoning packets

2 c. frozen stir-fry vegetable
     blend, thawed
2 c. water
2 T. green onion, sliced

Brown ground beef in a skillet over medium heat; drain. Stir in one
seasoning packet; remove beef from skillet. Combine noodles,
remaining seasoning packet, vegetables and water in skillet. Bring to a
boil; reduce heat to medium. Cover and simmer for 3 minutes, or until
noodles are tender, stirring occasionally. Return browned beef to
skillet; heat through. Stir in green onion and mix well.

Make brown & serve dinner rolls extra yummy. Before baking, brush with a little beaten egg and sprinkle with shredded Parmesan cheese and Italian seasoning.

Stroganoff Skillet

Serves 4

1 lb. ground beef
1 onion, chopped
10-3/4 oz. can cream of
    mushroom soup

8-oz. container sour cream
1 c. beef broth
1/2 c. water
3 c. wide egg noodles, uncooked

Brown ground beef and onion in a large skillet over medium heat; drain. Gradually blend in remaining ingredients. Bring to a boil. Reduce heat; cover and simmer for 10 minutes, or until noodles are tender.

For a terrific change of taste, try a fruit salsa in Salsa Ranch
Skillet. Peach, pineapple, red raspberry and cherry salsas
are all flavorful substitutions.

Salsa Ranch Skillet

Serves 4 to 6

1 lb. ground beef
1/2 c. sweet onion, chopped
1/2 c. green pepper, chopped
2.8-oz. pkg. ranch salad
    dressing mix
1 c. water

15-oz. can tomato sauce
16-oz. jar mild salsa
16-oz. can baked beans
8-oz. pkg. rotini pasta,
    uncooked
1 c. shredded Colby Jack cheese

Brown ground beef with onion and pepper in a large skillet over high heat; drain. Stir in dressing mix until thoroughly blended. Stir in water, tomato sauce, salsa and beans; bring to a boil. Add pasta; reduce to medium-low heat. Simmer for 12 to 15 minutes until pasta is tender, stirring occasionally. Remove from heat; sprinkle with cheese and let stand for 5 minutes, until cheese melts and sauce thickens.

Instead of serving traditional dinner rolls, bake up some sweet and tangy cranberry muffins. Just stir frozen cranberries into cornbread muffin mix and bake as directed on the package.

Cincinnati Skillet

Serves 4 to 6

1 lb. ground beef
1 T. garlic, minced
15-oz. can tomato sauce
14-1/2 oz. can diced tomatoes
3/4 t. ground cumin
3/4 t. dried oregano
1/2 t. cinnamon

4 c. zucchini, thickly sliced
4 c. yellow squash, thickly
  sliced
15-oz. jar pearl onions, drained
  and rinsed
10-oz. pkg. couscous, cooked

Brown ground beef with garlic in a large skillet over medium-high
heat; drain. Stir in tomato sauce, tomatoes, cumin, oregano and
cinnamon. Add remaining vegetables; mix well. Bring to a boil;
reduce heat, cover and simmer until zucchini and squash are tender,
about 10 to 12 minutes. Spoon over couscous to serve.

If mashed potatoes are on the dinner menu, whip in a teaspoon or so of baking powder and they'll be extra light and fluffy.

Speedy Supper

Serves 4 to 6

1 lb. ground beef, browned and
  drained
1/3 c. long-cooking rice,
  uncooked
1-oz. pkg. onion gravy mix
1/4 t. garlic salt
1-1/2 c. water
10-oz. pkg. frozen peas, thawed
8-oz. can sliced water
  chestnuts, drained
2.8-oz. can French fried onions
soy sauce to taste

Combine beef, rice, gravy mix, garlic salt and water to a large skillet.
Bring to a boil over medium-high heat. Reduce to low; cover and
simmer for 15 minutes. Stir in peas and water chestnuts; simmer
until rice is tender, about 10 additional minutes. Remove from heat;
toss in onions. Season with soy sauce before serving.

Keep the cowboy theme going when serving Wagon Wheel
Skillet. Line a cowboy hat with bandannas and fill with fresh
veggies, then slip a Mason jar of water and flowers inside a
cowboy boot for a whimsical centerpiece!

Wagon Wheel Skillet

Serves 5 to 6

1 T. dried, minced onion
1/2 c. milk
1-1/2 lbs. ground beef
1 egg, beaten
1/2 c. quick-cooking oats,
    uncooked
1 to 2 t. salt

1/4 t. pepper
browning and seasoning sauce
    to taste
1 c. spaghetti sauce with
    mushrooms
1 c. canned kidney beans,
    drained and rinsed

Soak onion in milk for 5 minutes; mix in beef, egg, oats, salt and pepper. Mound in a large skillet; score into 5 or 6 wedges. Brush top lightly with browning sauce; set aside. Combine spaghetti sauce and kidney beans; pour over meat mixture. Simmer, uncovered, until done, about 25 to 30 minutes.

Keep a pair of scissors in the kitchen to make quick work of
cutting tomatoes, shredding lettuce, chopping celery and snipping
fresh herbs. They're handy for opening packages too!

One-Pot Supper

Serves 4 to 6

1-1/2 lbs. ground beef
1/2 c. onion, chopped
10-3/4 oz. can cream of
    mushroom soup
3/4 c. milk
1 t. fresh parsley, chopped

1/8 t. pepper
8-oz. pkg. cream cheese, diced
15-1/4 oz. can corn, drained
8-oz. pkg. medium egg noodles,
    cooked

In a heavy Dutch oven, brown ground beef with onion; drain. Mix in soup and milk; stir until well blended. Add parsley, pepper and cream cheese; stir until cheese is melted. Stir in corn; heat through. Serve over cooked noodles.

Only using half an onion? Rub the remaining half with butter or olive oil, store in the fridge in a plastic zipping bag...it will stay fresh for weeks.

Fiesta Platter

Serves 6 to 8

1 lb. ground beef
1-1/4 oz. pkg. taco seasoning
    mix
14-1/2 oz. can tomatoes with
    chiles
10-1/2 oz. can chili without
    beans
16-oz. pkg. pasteurized process
    cheese spread, cubed

1 c. whipping cream
13-1/2 oz. pkg. tortilla chips
Garnish: shredded lettuce, diced
    tomatoes, sliced olives,
    chopped onion, sour cream,
    salsa

Brown ground beef in a large skillet over medium-high heat; drain. Add taco seasoning, tomatoes and chili; stir well. Reduce heat. Add cheese; stir until melted. Stir in whipping cream; mix well. Simmer over low heat for 10 to 15 minutes, stirring occasionally. Serve over tortilla chips; garnish with lettuce, tomatoes, olives, onion, sour cream and salsa.

Colanders can get sticky and hard to clean after draining pastas. To prevent this, coat the colander with a non-stick vegetable spray before using.

Skillet Spaghetti

Serves 4

1 lb. ground beef
1 onion, diced
2 14-1/2 oz. cans chicken broth
6-oz. can tomato paste
1/2 t. dried oregano
1/8 t. garlic powder

1/2 t. salt
1/4 t. pepper
8-oz. pkg. spaghetti, uncooked
  and broken
Garnish: grated Parmesan
  cheese

Brown ground beef and onion in a large skillet over medium heat.
Drain; return to skillet. Stir in broth, tomato paste and seasonings;
bring to a boil. Add spaghetti; reduce heat and simmer, stirring often,
for 10 to 15 minutes, until spaghetti is tender. Sprinkle with cheese.

INDEX

INDEX

How Did Gooseberry Patch Get Started?

Gooseberry Patch started in 1984 one day over the backyard fence in Delaware, Ohio. We were next-door neighbors who shared a love of collecting antiques, gardening and country decorating. Though neither of us had any experience (Jo Ann was a first-grade school teacher and Vickie, a flight attendant & legal secretary), we decided to try our hands at the mail-order business. Since we both had young children, this was perfect for us. We could work from our kitchen tables and keep an eye on the kids too! As our children grew, so did our "little" business. We moved into our own building in the country and filled the shelves to the brim with kitchenware, candles, gourmet goodies, enamelware, bowls and our very own line of cookbooks, calendars and organizers. We're so glad you're a part of our **Gooseberry Patch** family!

For a free copy of our **Gooseberry Patch**
catalog, write us, call us or visit us online at:

Gooseberry Patch
600 London Rd.
★ P.O. Box 190 ★
Delaware, OH 43015

1·800·854·6673
www.gooseberrypatch.com